A Classic Collection

A Child's Garden
of Prayer

Illustrations by Marilynn Barr

CONCORDIA PUBLISHING HOUSE · SAINT LOUIS

Library of Congress Cataloging-in-Publication Data

A child's garden of prayer
    p. cm.
ISBN 0-7586-0785-7
1. Prayers - - Juvenile literature.   I. Concordia Publishing House.
    BV212.C47 2005
    242' . 82 - - dc22   2004009899

2 3   4   5   6   7   8   9   10   14   13   12   11   10   09   08   07   06   05

I am a child of God.

My name is

Place
Your Photo
Here

Preface

Praying is a special way people talk to God. There are many different kinds of prayers. You can talk to Him about anything—anywhere—anytime. What do you talk to God about?

Some prayers praise God. One way to show praise is to tell God you love Him.

Most kind and loving Father in heaven,
I love You. For Jesus' sake. Amen.

Some prayers ask God to forgive you for the wrong things you do. We all sin. But God loves you and will forgive you for Jesus' sake.

Forgive me, heavenly Father, for the wrong I
have done. I ask in Jesus' name. Amen.

Some prayers thank God for all His wonderful gifts. There is so much to thank God for ... the world, the seasons, loved ones, homes, food, good weather, everything! But the best thing God gave was His only Son, Jesus, so we might have life with Him in heaven.

Thank You for everything, God—especially our
Savior, Jesus. Amen.

Some prayers ask God for help. God knows your needs, even before you know them. He knows when you are in trouble and is always willing to help. Ask God for help.

Protect me, God, from all harm. In the name of
Jesus I pray. Amen.

Some prayers ask God for guidance. Every day you are faced with decisions. Should I do this or that? Ask God to lead you in the right direction.

God, help me to do the right things and make the choices that will please You. In Jesus' name. Amen.

Some prayers ask God for things that you need. Sometimes you want something very much. But God decides, like any good parent, what is best for you to have. You ask God, but you have to wait patiently for His answer. Remember, God will give you everything you need, but not everything you want.

God, help me want what's good for me. Let Your will be done. For Jesus' sake. Amen.

You can also talk to God about others.

You can pray for a friend.

You can pray for an enemy.

You can pray for your loved ones.

You can pray for people you haven't met but know that they need help.

You can pray for other Christians.

You can pray for those who haven't come to know the meaning of God's plan for them.

You can pray about anything, anywhere, anytime. You can pray alone or with someone. At the table your family might say a prayer of thanks before eating a meal. You might pray with your friends in church or Sunday school. You might pray at special times set aside by the family, called devotions.

Sometimes you pray all alone. Some people kneel beside their bed. Some people talk to God outside in the sunshine.

It doesn't matter where you are, how you are dressed, or how you look. God listens to every prayer. So pray whenever you like; pray as long as you like; pray as often as you like. If prayers are said with faith in Jesus, that is enough for God.

(from *Prayer: Learning How to Talk to God*)

The Lord's Prayer

Our Father, who art in heaven,
    Hallowed be Thy name,
    Thy kingdom come,
    Thy will be done
        on earth as it is in heaven.
Give us this day our daily bread;
and forgive us our trespasses
    as we forgive those
    who trespass against us;
and lead us not into temptation,
    but deliver us from evil.
For Thine is the kingdom
    and the power and the glory
    forever and ever.
    Amen.

Prayers for Morning

I thank You, my heavenly Father, through Jesus Christ, Your dear Son, that You have kept me this night from all harm and danger; and I pray that You would keep me this day also from sin and every evil, that all my doings and life may please You. For into Your hands I commend myself, my body and soul, and all things. Let Your holy angel be with me, that the evil foe may have no power over me. Amen.

(Luther's Morning Prayer)

In the early morning,
With the sun's first rays,
All God's little children
Thank and pray and praise.
Always in Thy keeping,
Jesus, Savior dear,
Whether waking, sleeping,
Be Thou ever near. Amen.

(from *God's Children Pray*)

For this new morning and its light,
For rest and shelter of the night,
For health and food, for love and friends,
For everything Your goodness sends
I thank You, heavenly Father. Amen.

(from *Little Folded Hands*)

Jesus, gentle Shepherd,
Bless Thy lamb today;
Keep me in Thy footsteps,
Never let me stray.
Guard me through the daytime,
Every hour, I pray;
Keep my feet from straying
From the narrow way. Amen.
(from *Little Folded Hands*)

Jesus, help me all this day
In my work and in my play
Both to love and to obey. Amen.
(from *Little Folded Hands*)

Heavenly Father, hear my prayer;
Keep me in Thy loving care.
Guard me through the coming day
In my work and in my play.
Keep me pure and strong and true;
Help me, Lord, Thy will to do. Amen.
(from *Little Folded Hands*)

O blessed Lord, protect me
And my parents, graciously;
From sin defend and keep me free;
Help me a Christlike child to be. Amen.
(from *Little Folded Hands*)

Dear God, I thank You for this day
That's only just begun—
The pearly dew upon the grass,
The newly risen sun.
Be with me in the busy hours
And lay Your hand in mine.
Please let the path I walk be bright,
With loving deeds ashine.
Teach me to know You and to pray.
Dear God, I thank You for this day. Amen.

(from *God, I've Gotta Talk to You!*)

Savior, stay with me this day,
While I work and while I play.
I know that You love me true.
Help me show my love for You. Amen.

(from *All God's People Sing*, 206:2)

Prayers for Evening

I thank You, my heavenly Father, through Jesus Christ, Your dear Son, that You have graciously kept me this day; and I pray You would forgive me all my sins where I have done wrong, and graciously keep me this night. For into Your hands I commend myself, my body and soul, and all things. Let Your holy angel be with me, that the evil foe may have no power over me. Amen.

Luther's Evening Prayer

Now I lay me down to sleep;
I pray Thee, Lord, my soul to keep.
If I should die before I wake,
I pray Thee, Lord, my soul to take;
And this I ask for Jesus' sake. Amen.

(from *Little Folded Hands*)

Be near me, Lord Jesus!
I ask Thee to stay
Close by me forever
And love me, I pray.
Bless all the dear children
In Thy tender care,
And take us to heaven
To live with Thee there. Amen.

(from *Lutheran Worship*, 64:3)

Now the light has gone away;
Savior, listen while I pray,
Asking Thee to watch and keep
And to send me quiet sleep.

Jesus, Savior, wash away
All that has been wrong today;
Help me every day to be
Good and gentle, more like Thee.

Let my near and dear ones be
Always near and dear to Thee.
Oh, bring me and all I love
To Thy happy home above. Amen.
(from *Little Folded Hands*)

At the close of every day,
Lord, to Thee, I kneel and pray.
Look upon Thy little child,
Look in love and mercy mild;
Please forgive and wash away
All my naughtiness this day;
While I sleep and when awake,
Bless me for my Savior's sake. Amen.
(from *Little Folded Hands*)

Watch o'er this little child tonight,
Blest Savior from above,
And keep me till the morning light
Within Thine arms of love. Amen.
(from *Little Folded Hands*)

Forgive, O Lord, through Thy dear Son,
The wrongs that I this day have done;
That with the world, myself, and Thee
I, when I sleep, at peace may be. Amen.

(from *Little Folded Hands*)

Dear Father in heaven,
Look down from above;
Bless daddy and mommy,
And all whom I love.
May angels guard over
My slumbers, and when
The morning is breaking,
Awaken me. Amen.

(from *Little Folded Hands*)

Jesus, tender Shepherd, hear me,
Bless Thy little lamb tonight;
Through the darkness be Thou near me,
Keep me safe till morning light.

All this day Thy hand has led me,
And I thank Thee for Thy care;
Thou has warmed and clothed and fed me;
Listen to my evening prayer.

May my sins all be forgiven;
Bless the friends I love so well;
Take us all at last to heaven,
Happy there with Thee to dwell. Amen.

(from *Little Folded Hands*)

Dear Father, whom I cannot see,
Smile down from heaven on little me.
Let angels through the darkness spread
Their holy wings around my bed.
And keep me safe, because I am
My loving Shepherd's little lamb. Amen.
(from *Little Folded Hands*)

Good night, Lord Jesus,
Guard us in sleep;
Our souls and bodies
In Thy love keep.
Waking or sleeping,
Keep us in sight;
Dear gentle Savior,
Good night, good night. Amen.
(from *Little Folded Hands*)

Bless me as I fall asleep.
Send Your angels watch to keep. Amen.
(from *God's Children Pray*)

It's time for me to go to sleep.
Dear Jesus, now I pray:
Thank You, dear Lord, for all I've done.
I thank You for today. Amen.
(from *God's Children Pray*)

Lord Jesus, keep me in Thy sight
Through the coming hours of night.
Then when morning sunlight beams
Wake me, Lord, from sleepy dreams. Amen.
(from *God's Children Pray*)

The day is done;
O God the Son,
Look down upon
Thy little one!
O God of Light,
Keep me this night,
And send to me
Thy angels bright.
I need not fear
If Thou art near;
Thou art my Savior,
Kind and dear. Amen.

(from *God's Children Pray*)

Be our light in the darkness, O Lord, and in
Your great mercy defend us from all perils and
dangers of this night; for the love of Your only
Son, our Savior Jesus Christ. Amen.

(from *Lutheran Worship*, p. 267)

Thank You, God,
    For making the world and all that is in it.
Thank You, God,
    For making my wonderful body and mind.
Thank You, God,
    For my home, my parents, and
    all the people who love and
    care for me.
Thank You, God,
    For food to eat and clothes to wear
Thank You, God,

For leading me to know
Jesus, my Savior and Lord.
Thank You, God,
For Baptism and the gifts
of the Holy Spirit.
Thank You, God,
For everything. Amen.

The night is dark and silent now;
Make darkness good and silence rest.
Lord, let my sleep tonight endow
Me with Thy peace and blessedness;
And if the morning comes to me.
Grant me laughter, life, and Thee. Amen.
(from *God, I've Gotta Talk to You!*)

All praise to Thee, my God, this night
For all the blessings of the light.
Keep me, oh, keep me, King of kings,
Beneath Thine own almighty wings.
Forgive me, Lord, for Thy dear Son,
The ill that I this day have done;
That with the world, myself, and Thee,
I, ere I sleep, at peace may be. Amen.
(from *Lutheran Worship*, 484:1,2)

Savior, stay with me tonight.
Send Your love and peace and light.
Keep me safe within Your love,
'Til You take me home above. Amen.
(from *All God's People Sing*, 206:3)

For Naptime

It's time to nap, I'd rather play;
The day's just partly done.
Be with me now, dear Jesus,
And I'll wake to have more fun! Amen.

(from *God's Children Pray*)

Table Prayers

Before Meals

Come, Lord Jesus, be our Guest,
And let Thy gifts to us be blessed. Amen.
God is great, and God is good,
And we thank Him for our food;
By His hand we all are fed;
Give us, Lord, our daily bread. Amen.

(from *Little Folded Hands*)

God bless this food,
And bless us all,
For Jesus' sake. Amen.
(from *Little Folded Hands*)

Be present at our table, Lord;
Be here and everywhere adored.
Thy children bless, and grant that we
May feast in paradise with Thee. Amen.
(from *Little Folded Hands*)

Jesus, bless what Thou hast given,
Feed our souls with bread from heaven;
Guide and lead us by Thy love
Until we reach our home above. Amen.
(from *Little Folded Hands*)

For food and all Thy gifts of love,
We give Thee thanks and praise.
Look down, O Jesus, from above,
And bless us all our days. Amen.
(from *Little Folded Hands*)

Lord God, heavenly Father, bless us and these
Thy gifts, which we receive from Thy bountiful goodness,
through Jesus Christ, our Lord. Amen.

Grant us Thy grace, O Lord, that, whether we eat
or drink, or whatever we do, we may do it all in Thy
name and to Thy glory. Amen.
(from *Little Folded Hands*)

Our hands we fold,
Our heads we bow;
For food and drink
We thank Thee now. Amen.
(from *God's Children Pray*)

Bless this food,
Dear Lord, we pray.
Make us thankful
Every day. Amen.
(from *God's Children Pray*)

Father, make me thankful
For food that may not be
The food I think is best to eat,
But still is good for me. Amen.
(from *God's Children Pray*)

Heavenly Father, let me see
All the ways that You bless me.
Thank You for the food I'm fed;
Thank You for my daily bread. Amen.
(from *God's Children Pray*)

Now we bow our heads to pray;
Thank You for this food today.
Now we fold our hands and say,
"Thank You, Lord, in every way." Amen.
(from *God's Children Pray*)

Dear God, our thanks for everything:
The sun that shines, the birds that sing,
The flowers that bloom, the wind that blows,
The food and drink that help us grow.

We thank You for the bread we eat,
For all the vegetables and meat.
We thank You for dessert, so yummy;

We eat it 'til it fills our tummies.
We thank You for this family,
Big or small 'though we may be.
Thank You for this meal, we pray;
Please bless us all in every way. Amen.
(from *More Songs of Gladness*)

Our health is given by this food;
Our food, dear Lord, comes by Thy grace.
Our thanks we offer in return
At every meal, in every place. Amen.
(from *God, I've Gotta Talk to You!*)

Dear God, I thank You for this food
As well as I am able.
Please bless it, Father, to our use,
And be our Guest at table. Amen.
(from *God, I've Gotta Talk to You!*)

After Meals

We thank You, Lord, for food and drink, through Jesus Christ. Amen.

(from *Little Folded Hands*)

Dear Father in heaven, accept our thanks for this food and for all Thy blessings, through Jesus Christ. Amen.

(from *Little Folded Hands*)

We thank Thee, Lord God, heavenly Father, through Jesus Christ, our Lord, for all Thy benefits, who lives and reigns forever and ever. Amen.

(from *Little Folded Hands*)

For health and food, for love and friends,
For everything Thy goodness sends,
Father in heaven, we thank Thee. Amen.

(from *Little Folded Hands*)

We thank Thee for these gifts, O Lord;
Now feed our souls, too, with Thy Word.
Amen.
(from *Little Folded Hands*)

The Lord is good to all, and His tender mercies are over all His works. Bless the Lord, O my soul, and all that is within me, bless His holy name. Bless the Lord, O my soul, and forget not all His benefits. Amen.
(from *Little Folded Hands*)

For food and drink and happy days,
Accept our gratitude and praise;
In serving others, Lord, may we
Express our thankfulness to Thee. Amen.
(from *Little Folded Hands*)

Thank You for the world so sweet.
Thank You for the food we eat.
Thank You for the birds that sing.
Thank You, God, for everything. Amen.
(from *God's Children Pray*)

We thank You, Lord, for happy hearts,
For sun and rainy weather.
We thank You for the food we eat
And that we are together. Amen.
(from *God's Children Pray*)

Prayers for Others

Bless me, dearest Lord; I pray
That I may bless someone today.
Show me how to share Your joy
With every girl and every boy. Amen.
(from *God's Children Pray*)

O Jesus, so kind; O Jesus, so mild;
You care for me, a little child.
Your love surrounds me day to day;
You bend and listen when I pray.

O Jesus, so kind; O Jesus, so mild;
Be always near Your little child.
Protect all other children, too,
And help us grow to be like You.
O Jesus, so kind; O Jesus, so mild. Amen.
(from *God's Children Pray*)

Dear Father in heaven,
Look down from above,
Bless Papa and Mama
And all whom I love.
May angels guard over
My slumbers, and when
The morning is breaking,
Awake me. Amen.
(from *A Child's Garden of Prayer*)

There are so many people
who show me love and care
It's for all those special people
That I come to You in prayer.
Dear Lord, I ask Your blessing
Upon these people that I love.
Watch over them, and guide them;
Lead them in Your path of love.
Amen.

Dear Jesus, I love You,
I thank You, I praise.
Dear Jesus, my family
To You today I raise.
Forgive them, protect them,
Love them, I pray.
And Jesus, please bless them
In all they do and say. Amen.

Dear God, I pray to You today
For my friends and me.
I pray that Jesus' little lambs
are what we'll always be.
Amen.

Lord, bless my playmates, this I pray.
Bless us in all we do or say.
And when we part, oh, may we still
Be safely kept from every ill. Amen.

(from *A Child's Garden of Prayer*)

Lord, bless the little children
In all the world, we pray;
Help everyone to love Thee,
And keep them in Thy way. Amen.

(from *Little Folded Hands*)

Dear Jesus, You are our forever Friend. You even laid down Your life for us. Thank You for Your promise to be with us always. Help each of us to be a friend to others, especially those who are lonely. In Your name we pray. Amen.

(from *Little Visits: 365 Family Devotions.* Volume 1)

Dear Jesus, help us share Your love and our possessions with others. Give each of us a generous heart because of Your generous blessings to us every day. Amen.

(from *Little Visits: 365 Family Devotions.* Volume 1)

Heavenly Father, help us know what to say or do so Your message of love and forgiveness can make a difference in someone's life. Make us strong when we're afraid to speak to someone about You. In Jesus' name we pray. Amen.

(from *Little Visits: 365 Family Devotions.* Volume 1)

Dear God, thank You for giving us people to take care of us. We know that loving parents are a gift from You. Help everyone in our family love and forgive one another for Jesus' sake. Amen.

(from *Little Visits: 365 Family Devotions.* Volume 1)

Lord, gather all Your children,
Wherever they may be,
And lead them on to heaven
To live eternally
With You, our loving Father,
And Christ, our Brother dear,
Whose Spirit guards and gives us
The joy to persevere. Amen.

(from *Lutheran Worship*, 320:6)

God, bless Your helpers, wise and meek.
God, bless them now and through the week.

God, bless the preachers of Your Word.
May Your voice in theirs be heard.
God, bless our teachers also who
Help us learn of what You do.

Bless those who pray and those who sing:
Loud and clear hosannas ring.
Oh, bless all those who worship You,
Moms and dads and children, too.

God, bless Your helpers, wise and bold.
God, make their work as good as gold. Amen.

(from *More Songs of Gladness*)

Prayers for School and Church

Dear Lord Jesus, go with me to school today, and make me obedient to my teachers. Help me to learn with pleasure whatever I am taught, so I may honor and serve Thee all my days. Amen.

(from *Little Folded Hands*)

Thank You, dear God, for the many teachers You have given us. Help us listen so we may learn lessons we need to know for our physical life and especially for eternal life with You and Your Son. In His name we pray. Amen.

(from *Little Visits: 365 Family Devotions.* Volume 1)

Dear God, my heavenly Father,
Bless me at school today,
And help me learn my lessons;
In Jesus' name I pray. Amen.
(from *Little Folded Hands*)

Assembled in our school once more,
O Lord, Thy blessing we implore;
We meet to work, to sing, to pray;
Be with us, then, throughout this day. Amen.
(from *Little Folded Hands*)

Father, bless our school today;
Be in all we do or say;
Be in ev'ry song we sing;
Ev'ry prayer to Thee we bring.

Jesus, well-beloved Son,
May Thy will by us be done,
Come and meet with us today;
Teach us, Lord, Thyself, we pray. Amen.
(from *Little Folded Hands*)

Dear Savior, bless the children
Who've gathered here today;
Oh, send Thy Holy Spirit,
And teach us how to pray.

Lord, bless the work we're doing,
Oh, bless our gifts, though small,
And hear our prayer for Jesus' sake,
Who died to save us all. Amen.
(from *Little Folded Hands*)

We thank Thee, heav'nly Father,
For all that we have heard;
Teach us to love our Savior
And to obey Thy Word. Amen.
(from *Little Folded Hands*)

Father, we thank You for Your Word,
And for the lessons we have heard;
Be with us as we homeward go;
Help us to do the things we know. Amen.
(from *Little Folded Hands*)

Dear Jesus, bless each little child,
And keep us all, we pray,
Safe in Thy loving care until
Another holy day. Amen.
(from *Little Folded Hands*)

Lord, we bring our off'ring;
Use it that Your Word
May be told to children
Who have never heard.

Some are in our homeland,
Some across the sea.
May they learn of Jesus:
This our prayer shall be. Amen.
(from *Little Folded Hands*)

Jesus, bless the gifts we bring Thee,
Give them something sweet to do;
May they help someone to love Thee;
Jesus, may we love Thee, too. Amen.
(from *Little Folded Hands*)

Savior, use the gift I lay
Humbly at Thy feet today;
May it bring some child to Thee,
There to live eternally. Amen.

(from *A Child's Garden of Prayer*)

Lord Jesus, bless the pastor's word
Upon my heart, I pray;
That after all is said and heard
I gladly may obey. Amen.

(from *A Child's Garden of Prayer*)

The church bells ring
Within the steeple.
"Now's the hour,"
they tell the people.

The church's doors
Are open wide
So you and I
Can come inside

And worship Him
This holy day:
"Praise You!" [I] sing;
"Amen," [I] pray.

(adapted from *More Songs of Gladness*)

Lord God, thank You for giving me my abilities. Help me develop them as I go to school each day and prepare to serve You with my life. Bless my school, my teachers, and my classmates. For Jesus' sake. Amen.

(from *Little Visits: 365 Family Devotions.* Volume 2)

Prayers for Illness

Lord Jesus, You are always good
To everyone in pain;
Please think of me while I am ill,
And make me well again. Amen.
(from *Little Folded Hands*)

Dear Father in heaven, Your child is sick. Have mercy on me, and if it be Your will, give me health and strength, and keep me cheerful, through faith in Jesus, my Lord and Savior. Amen.
(from *Little Folded Hands*)

Lord Jesus, have mercy on my (mother, father, brother, sister) and make (her, him) well again soon, if it be Your will. You can do all things; and I know that You love us. More than anything else, keep us as Your children, and take us to heaven, for Your name's sake. Amen.

(from *Little Folded Hands*)

Faithful Shepherd, feed me
In the pastures green;
Faithful Shepherd, lead me
Where Thy steps are seen.
In my sickness help me
As Thou thinkest best,
Keep me close beside Thee,
Give me peace and rest. Amen.

(from *Little Folded Hands*)

I don't feel well; this is no fun.
Why am I sick today?
Dear Jesus, help me know You're here;
With me You'll always stay. Amen.

(from *God's Children Pray*)

Lord, show Your tender feeling;
For sickness give Your healing;
To minds, when dark thoughts frighten,
Come with Your joy, bring light in. Amen.

(from *Lutheran Worship*, 184:5)

Hear my prayer, Lord, for the ill:
Encourage them while they lie still
And give their restless spirits rest.
Lead them through the painful night,

Through fevers, needles, dreams, and fright;
Help their bodies, their spirits bless. Amen.
(from *God, I've Gotta Talk to You!*)

My body Thou hast healed again,
My spirit now restore;
Thy praises, Savior, I will sing,
Thy holy name adore. Amen.
(from *Little Folded Hands*)

Thy name I praise
In this glad hour,
For Thou has healed
Me by Thy power.
Lord, let me serve
Thee day by day
And never from
Thy pathway stray. Amen.
(from *Little Folded Hands*)

Prayers for Special Days

Birthdays

O Jesus, send Thy tender love
Upon me, please, today.
On this, my birthday, give me grace
A special prayer to say.
Few are my candles, few are my years;
So let my promise be
That all the years that I may live
I'll love and worship Thee. Amen.
(from *Little Folded Hands*)

We thank the Lord who kept you
All through the passing year;
He put His arms around you
And gave you health and cheer.

Now we will pray together
That He will keep you still
And make the next year happy
And help you do His will. Amen.
(from *Little Folded Hands*)

Dear Jesus, now my thanks I say
For giving me this nice birthday. Amen.
(from *God's Children Pray*)

Thank You, God, for sky and sea.
Thank You, God, for making me.

You gave me lungs so I could breathe.

You gave me a nose so I could sneeze.
You gave me a mind so I could think.
You gave me eyes so I could blink.

You gave me a home, my mom and dad,
And friends and pets. And am I glad!
You gave me a heart that beats in love
For things on earth and You above.

Thank You, God, for sky and sea.
Thank You, God, for making me. Amen.

(from *More Songs of Gladness*)

New Baby

Dear Jesus,
You gave me a new baby,
All little, noisy, warm.
Be with my little baby,
And keep us both from harm.

I know You love this baby.
I know You love me, too.
Help me to act as a child of Yours
In what I say and do. Amen.

(from *God's Children Pray*)

What a miracle we are given
From the God of earth and heaven;
He lends us this baby to bless our daily lives!
We thank You, dearest Father,
We your sons and daughters
How could we ever realize

Such a treasure, Your love without measure,
Come to us out of the skies!

Rest now, little one;
Life's adventure is just begun.
You are surrounded by all of us here,
And, most of all, by Him
Whose glory the angels sing:
God, our Maker and King! Amen.

(by John Paquet)

New Year's Day

Dear God, thank You for Your gift of a new year. Help us begin each day with You. In the name of Jesus, our Lord and Savior. Amen.

(from *Little Visits: 365 Family Devotions.* Volume 1)

Valentine's Day

A day of hearts,
A day of love,
Sent to us
From You above.
Thanks, Jesus. Amen.

(from *God's Children Pray*)

God of love, help us love others as You have loved us. In Jesus' name. Amen.

(from *Little Visits: 365 Family Devotions.* Volume 1)

Easter

Dear Jesus,
I'm working hard to learn about
What happened Easter Day,
When Mary went to the tomb
And heard the angel say:
"He is not here. He's risen!
Now tell to one and all."
And Mary ran right down the road.
"He's risen!" they heard her call.
Help me to learn and understand
What Easter's all about
So, when the people greet today,
I too can sing and shout:
Alleluia!
Thank You, Lord. Amen.

(from *God's Children Pray*)

The joyous time of Easter comes
Always during the spring
When, following the winter's chill,
[I] hear the robins sing.
Now everywhere [I] look it seems
That fresh, new life is seen—
From budding trees to crawly worms,
And many sprouts of green.
Praise God for it is wonderful
That Jesus came to earth,
Then died, but rose to live again,
So we could have new birth! ...

God sacrificed His only Son
To save us from our sin;
And so we have eternal life,
Since we believe in Him! Amen.

(adapted from *My Happy Easter Book*)

O Lord of all, with us abide
In this our joyful Eastertide.
From every weapon death can wield
Thine own redeemed forever shield. Amen.

(from *The Children's Hymnal, 50:3*)

Jesus, King of Glory, throned above the sky,
Jesus, tender Savior, hear Thy children cry.
Pardon our transgressions, cleanse us from our sin;
By Thy Spirit help us heav'nly life to win.
Jesus, King of Glory, throned above the sky,
Jesus, tender Savior, hear Thy children cry.

(from *The Children's Hymnal, 54:1*)

Mother's Day

Lord God, thank You for Mom and for all the things she does for our family. We are especially thankful that she has told us about You and Your love. In Jesus' name. Amen.

(from *Little Visits: 365 Family Devotions.* Volume 1.)

Dear God in highest heaven,
How can we thank You
Nearly as much as we ought to
For such a wonderful mother?
When it comes to caring for us,
After You, she's number two!

She loves us like no other.
By her example we understand
What it means to be formed
In the palm of Your hand.
Thanks, God, for Mom! Amen.
(by John Paquet)

Memorial Day

Dear heavenly Father, we are all called to serve in Your kingdom on earth. Some people are called to serve by being in the armed forces. And sometimes they lose their lives in service to their country. Thank You, God, for sending people who are willing to die to protect us. Let us always remember their bravery. And let us always remember with thankful hearts that Your Son, Jesus, died to save us. In His holy name. Amen.

Father's Day

When lifting our eyes to You,
Father and Maker of us all,
We sing out words of praise and thanks
However plain and small,
But especially for fathers
Like the one You've given me,
Whose heart pours out
With acts of love,
A joy for all to see.
Thanks, God, for Dad,
Sincerely! Amen.
(by John Paquet)

July Fourth

Dear loving God, lead each of us to work in Your kingdom according to Your plan for us. In Jesus' name. Amen.

(from *Little Visits: 365 Family Devotions.* Volume 2)

Labor Day

Dear Jesus, bless all of the workers in our country. In Your name we pray. Amen.

(from *Little Visits: 365 Family Devotions.* Volume 2)

Thanksgiving

It doesn't seem like a holiday,
I don't get anything new.
But all year long the love I get
Comes because of You. Amen.

(from *God's Children Pray*)

All praise and thanks to God
The Father now be given,
The Son, and Him who reigns
With them in highest heaven,
The one eternal God,
Whom earth and heav'n adore;
For thus it was, is now,
And shall be evermore.

(from *Lutheran Worship* 443:3)

Christmas

Ah, dearest Jesus, holy Child,
Make Thee a bed, soft, undefiled,
Within my heart, that it may be
A quiet chamber kept for Thee. Amen.
(from *A Child's Garden of Prayer*)

Long ago in Bethlehem
A little King was born.
Dear God, You sent Your Son to earth
That frosty Christmas morn.
You sent Him here to save the world
From sin and death and pain.
Dear God, I ask that in my heart
Your King will ever reign. Amen.
(from *Prayers for Little People*)

Two thousand years have passed, but still
We celebrate His birth—
The baby Jesus sent by God
To save us all on earth.
Thank You, God, for sending us

The gift of Your true Son,
For Jesus is the greatest gift
You gave to everyone! Amen.

(from *My Happy Birthday Book*)

King of earth and heaven too,
Earth could find no room for You.
Thank You for that Christmas Day
When You came here anyway.
In Your name I pray. Amen.

(from *My Christmas Prayer Book*)

Help me hear that news today.
Help me hear the angel say,
"Christ is born for you and me.
Christ is born, and we are free."
In Your name I pray. Amen.

(from *My Christmas Prayer Book*)

Angels sang, and I will too,
"Glory, glory, Lord, to You!"
Help me sing of Jesus' birth.
Help me work for peace on earth.
In Your name I pray. Amen.

(from *My Christmas Prayer Book*)

Shepherds say and shepherds told
On that Christmas day of old.
Yes, I know the story well.
Help me, Lord, to gladly tell.
In Your name I pray. Amen.

(from *My Christmas Prayer Book*)

O holy Child of Bethlehem,
Descend to us, we pray;
Cast out our sin,
And enter in,
Be born in us today.
We hear the Christmas angels
The great glad tidings tell;
Oh, come to us,
Abide with us,
Our Lord Immanuel! Amen.

(from *All God's People Sing*, 183:4)

General Prayers

Jesus, help my eyes to see
All the good Thou sendest me.
Jesus, help my ears to hear
Calls for help from far and near.
Jesus, help my feet to go
In the way that Thou wilt show.
Jesus, help my hands to do
All things loving, kind, and true.
Jesus, may I helpful be,
Growing daily more like Thee. Amen.
(from *Little Folded Hands*)

Lord, bless the little children
In all the world, we pray;
Help everyone to love Thee,
And keep them in Thy way. Amen.
(from *Little Folded Hands*)

God the Father, bless us;
God the Son, defend us;
God the Spirit, keep us
Now and evermore. Amen.
(from *Little Folded Hands*)

Blest Savior dear, be always near;
Keep me from evil, harm, and fear. Amen.
(from *Little Folded Hands*)

Dear Jesus,
I love You. Amen.
(from *God's Children Pray*)

Jesus, my Savior, kind and true,
Jesus, my Savior, I love You. Amen.
(from *God's Children Pray*)

I'm Your child, for You love me.
You died and rose so I could be
All full of hope and joy and love
Which come from You, my Lord, above. Amen.
(from *God's Children Pray*)

God, be in our heads
    And in our understanding.
God, be in our eyes
    And in our looking.
God, be in our mouths
    And in our speaking.
God, be in our hearts
    And in our loving.
God, be in our bodies
    And in our doing.

God, be in us; be in us always.
    In Jesus' name. Amen.
(from *God's Children Pray*)

Lord, teach a little child to pray,
And, oh, accept my prayer;
Thou hearest all the words I say,
For Thou art everywhere.

A little sparrow cannot fall
Unnoticed, Lord, by Thee;
And though I am so young and small,
Thou carest still for me.

Teach me to do Thy will today,
And when I sin, forgive;
Grant that, for Jesus' sake, I may
With Thee forever live. Amen.
(from *A Child's Garden of Prayer*)

Creator God, we praise You for having wonderfully made us to be so special. We thank You for Your continuing care of us. Help us appreciate the uniqueness of each person as a member of Your family. In Jesus' name. Amen.
(from *Little Visits: 365 Family Devotions.* Volume 1)

Lord Jesus, thank You for planting Your Word in our hearts. Give us Your Holy Spirit so we can grow strong in You and bear the fruit of good works. In Your name we pray. Amen.
(from *Little Visits: 365 Family Devotions.* Volume 1)

Dear Father, help us to remember that no matter where we are, people see us. Inspire us to do and say things that will give You glory. For Jesus' sake, forgive us when we do wrong. In His name we pray. Amen.

(from *Little Visits: 365 Family Devotions.* Volume 1)

Abba Father, You loved us even before we were born and You will love us forever. You prepared a place in heaven for us, and You even planned a way for us to get there. Thank You, Lord, for sending Jesus. In His name we pray. Amen.

(from *Little Visits: 365 Family Devotions.* Volume 1)

Lord Jesus, reign in us, we pray,
And make us Yours alone,
Who with the Father ever are
And Holy Spirit, one. Amen.

(from *Lutheran Worship,* 77:6)

Lord Jesus Christ, be present now;
Our hearts in true devotion bow.
Your Spirit send with light divine,
And let Your truth within us shine. Amen.

(from *Lutheran Worship,* 201:1)

Yours forever, God of love!
Hear us from Your throne above.
Yours forever may we be
Here and in eternity. Amen.

(from *Lutheran Worship,* 256:1)

We give You but Your own
In any gifts we bring;
All that we have is Yours alone,
A trust from You, our King. Amen.

(from *Lutheran Worship,* 405:1)

Sometimes it's very clear to me
Exactly what I'm going to be:
Doctor, lawyer, merchantman,
Astronaut or fireman
But now and then I get confused;
I'm not quite sure just what to choose.
I know I won't go far alone,
So, help me, Lord, before I'm grown. Amen.

(from *God, I've Gotta Talk to You ... Again!*)

Lord Jesus, help me be kind and loving to all people I meet, no matter who they are. Show me how to love them just as You love me. Amen.

(from *Little Visits: 365 Family Devotions.* Volume 2.)

Dear heavenly Father, thank You for giving us people who love and care for us. Thank You, too for making us part of Your family. Forgive us for the times we do not show our love for You and our family. Help us live as Your children in all we do and say. In Your Son's name we pray. Amen.

(from *Little Visits: 365 Family Devotions.* Volume 2.)

Let me learn of Jesus;
He is kind to me;
Once He died to save me,
Nailed upon the tree.

When I go to Jesus,
He will hear me pray,
Make me pure and holy,
Take my sins away.

Oh, how good is Jesus!
May He hold my hand
And at last receive me
To a better land. Amen.
(from *All God's People Sing*, 156:1,2,4)

When I'm Thankful

We thank You, God for sunshine
And for the gentle rain,
We thank You for the harvest fields
Of waving, golden grain.
We thank You for the flour,
For bread, and all our food;
We thank You, God for everything;
You are so kind and good. Amen.
(from *Little Folded Hands*)

Jesus, tender Savior,
Thou hast died for me;
Make me very thankful
In my heart to Thee.
When the sad, sad story
Of Thy grief I read,
Make me very sorry
For my sins indeed. Amen.
(from *Little Folded Hands*)

God made the sun,
And God made the tree;
God made the mountains,
And God made me.

I thank You, O God,
For the sun and the tree,
For making the mountains
And for making me. Amen.
(from *Little Folded Hands*)

Jesus, lead me day by day
Ever in Thine own sweet way;
Teach me to be pure and true;
Show me what I ought to do.

When in danger, make me brave;
Make me know that Thou dost save;
Keep me safe by Thy dear side;
Let me in Thy love abide. Amen.
(from *Little Folded Hands*)

I thank You, Jesus, for the night
And for the pleasant morning light,
For rest and food and loving care
And all that makes the world so fair.
Help me to do the things I should,
To be to others kind and good,
In all I do at work or play,
To grow more loving every day. Amen.
(from *God's Children Pray*)

For warm, safe homes,
For clothes to wear,
For food to eat and food to share—
Thank You, Jesus. Amen.
(from *God's Children Pray*)

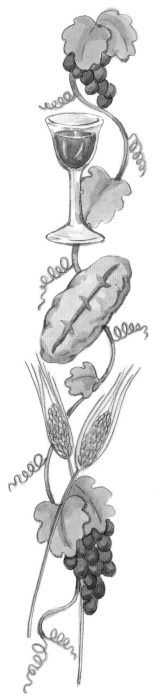

Thank You, God, for friends at play.
Thank You for each brand new day.
Thank You for the morning light.
Thank You for our beds at night. Amen.
(from *God's Children Pray*)

We give You but Your own
In any gifts we bring;
All that we have is Yours alone,
A trust from You, our King.
(from *Lutheran Worship 405:1*)

Thank You for the fluffy clouds
That float up in the sky.
Thank You for this world so good
That shines inside my eyes.
Thank You, Lord, for all my toys.
(from *Prayers for the Very Young Child*)

We thank You, Lord God, heavenly Father, for all Your benefits, through Jesus Christ, our Lord, who lives and reigns with You and the Holy Spirit forever and ever. Amen.
(from *Luther's Small Catechism*)

Lord God, heavenly Father, bless us and these Thy gifts which we receive from Thy bountiful goodness, through Jesus Christ, our Lord. Amen.
(from *Luther's Small Catechism*)

I thank You, Father, for my friends,
Who are so close to me.
We laugh and play; at school we work
So very busily.

I thank You for my special Friend,
Who lays His hand in mine
And looks at me with loving eyes,
Like candle flames ashine.

I thank You for His gracious love,
Which never has an end.
I thank You, Father, for Your Son,
My Brother and my Friend. Amen.
(from *God, I've Gotta Talk to You!*)

The sky is blue, the grass is green,
The flowers are in bloom.
The trees reach up into the sky,
The clouds look like balloons.

I am so happy to be here
Surrounded by Your love,
For all the things my eyes can see
Were sent from You above.

I cannot make a tree or cloud;
I cannot make the sea.
I'm happy that You made them, Lord,
And that You care for me. Amen.
(from *God, I've Gotta Talk to You ... Again!*)

Dear God, You made the mountains high;
You made the bubbly seas.
You made the pretty butterflies
And busy bumble bees.

You made the tiny grains of sand;
You made the big tall trees.
And then, Lord, with Your loving hands
You made a child named me. Amen.

(from *God, I've Gotta Talk to You ... Again!*)

My Creator, You give us everything in due season. Thank
You for showing us Your love in the sun and the rain, the flow-
ers and the snow, the blowing winds and the falling leaves.
Thank You most of all for Jesus. Amen.

(from *Little Visits: 365 Family Devotions.* Volume 2.)

Dear Jesus, thank You for the gift of friendship. Help me
appreciate the differences between my friends and me. Thank
You for being my best Friend. Amen.

(from *Little Visits: 365 Family Devotions* Volume 2.)

When I'm Happy

Lord God, thank You for all the things
that made us happy today. Fill our hearts
with joy each day and help us be mindful of
the blessings You surprise us with each day.
In Your name we pray. Amen.

(from *Little Visits: 365 Family Devotions.* Volume 1)

[You are] giving and forgiving,
Ever blessing, ever blest,
Wellspring of the joy of living,
Oceandepth of happy rest!
[You] our Father, Christ our brother,
All who live in love are Thine;
Teach us how to love each other,

Lift us to the joy divine! Amen.
(from *All God's People Sing*, 147:3)

In You is gladness
Amid all sadness,
Jesus, sunshine of my heart.
By You are given
The gifts of heaven.
You the true Redeemer are. Amen.
(adapted from *Lutheran Worship*, 442:1)

This is the day the LORD has made; let us rejoice and be glad in it (Psalm 118:24). Amen.

When I'm Sad

It's not so easy growing up
When things don't go my way.
Remind me patience and a smile
Will brighten up my day.

But even when I make mistakes,
I know You'll always be
My Jesus, my forgiving Lord,
Because You do love me. Amen.
(from *God's Children Pray*)

Sometimes I sit and worry
When I've done something bad.
I hide my tears and try to smile,
But worries make me sad.

Help me remember, Jesus,
That You will care for me

Through loving people, angels, too.
With me You'll always be. Amen.

(from *God's Children Pray*)

Dear Jesus, You know that sin brings so much sadness into the world. That's the whole reason You came—to live a life without sin and to suffer and die for all sins. Thank You for being our friend. Help us follow Your example and reach out to others who are hurting because of sin. In Your name we pray. Amen.

(from *Little Visits: 365 Family Devotions*. Volume 1)

Dear Jesus, thank You for cheering us up when we're feeling sad. Teach us what we need to know about You and Your love for us so we can deal with the disappointments and problems we face. We pray in Your powerful name. Amen.

(from *Little Visits: 365 Family Devotions*. Volume 1)

Dear Jesus, help us look to You in times of sorrow. Help us remember Your promise of love and support. We trust that in You we will find the joy that lasts. Amen.

(from *Little Visits: 365 Family Devotions*. Volume 1)

O Lord, we give thanks unto You
For all the good things that You do.

The winter You turn into springtime.
The rainstorm You turn into sunshine.
The tadpoles You turn into green frogs.
Small puppies You make into dogs.

The night You turn into the day.
Our sad times You turn into gay.

Boxes and strings become toys.
It's playtime for girls and boys.

How happy we are! How glad!
You turn into joy what is sad! Amen.
(from *More Songs of Gladness*)

Draw us to You, Each day anew.
Let us depart with gladness That we may be
Forever free From sorrow, grief, and sadness. Amen.
(from *Lutheran Worship*, 153:2)

When I'm Frightened

Jesus, I'm a little frightened.
I don't know what to do.
Help me know You're with me.
Help me, Lord, to trust in You. Amen.
(from *Prayers for the Very Young Child*)

Dear Father, often we're afraid when bad things happen.
Because You gave Your only Son for us, You will freely give us
everything else we need. Help us remember that You are
always with us, always helping us. In Jesus' name. Amen.
(from *Little Visits: 365 Family Devotions*. Volume 1)

Heavenly Father, thank You for sending Jesus, who gives us
hope in the middle of problems and who promises to come
again to take away all pain and problems. In His name. Amen.
(from *Little Visits: 365 Family Devotions*. Volume 1)

Dear God, thank You for loving us. When we feel afraid,
help us remember that You forgive us and protect us. We are
safe in Your care. In Jesus' holy name. Amen.
(from *Little Visits: 365 Family Devotions*. Volume 1)

Dear Jesus, thank You for protecting us from dangers of all kinds, especially the power of sin, death, and the devil. We know Your angels guard us every day. Help us make good decisions and do what is right. In Your name we pray. Amen.

(from *Little Visits: 365 Family Devotions.* Volume 1)

Dear God, sometimes we feel afraid. Help us trust You and know that You love us and will help us in every situation. Thanks for watching over us each and every day. In Jesus' name. Amen.

(from *Little Visits: 365 Family Devotions.* Volume 1)

Dear Father, sometimes we get frightened by the force of the weather. Heavy rain and strong winds make us realize how weak we are. Help us to trust in the power of Your love to give us protection. In Jesus' name we pray. Amen.

(from *Little Visits: 365 Family Devotions.* Volume 1)

Dear Father, You know everything about us. You know when we are afraid and need Your protection. Help us to trust in Your strength, confident that You love us, forgive us, and care for us. In Jesus' name. Amen.

(from *Little Visits: 365 Family Devotions.* Volume 1)

Dear Jesus, there are so many expectations put on each of us. Sometimes we feel afraid that we won't succeed. Give us the courage to try, and help us to trust that You will be with us in our successes and our failures. In Your name we pray. Amen.

(from *Little Visits: 365 Family Devotions.* Volume 1)

Lord, take my hand and lead me
Upon life's way;
Direct, protect, and feed me

From day to day.
Without Your grace and favor I go astray;
So take my hand, O Savior,
And lead the way.

Lord, when the tempest rages,
I need not fear;
For You, the Rock of Ages,
Are always near.
Close by Your side abiding,
I fear no foe,
For when Your hand is guiding,
In peace I go. Amen.
(from *Lutheran Worship*, 512:1, 2)

Sometimes I am frightened too.
Help me, Lord, remember You.
Take away my silly fright.
I am Yours. I'll be all right.
In Your name I pray. Amen.
(from *My Christmas Prayer Book*)

When I'm Lonely

Dear Jesus, heaven is our home because of Your gift of
salvation. Help us get through difficult days because of Your
promise of rest. Wrap us in the comfort of Your eternal love.
Amen.
(from *Little Visits: 365 Family Devotions*. Volume 1)

Dear Jesus, You were once alone;
You know my feelings to the bone.
Then be my Friend, make me Your own,

Love me, love me; be here, be kind,
And always keep me in Your mind. Amen.

(from *God, I've Gotta Talk to You!*)

Good Father, how comforting to know that You are with me! Help me turn to You in every lonely time of my life. Thank You for being here right now to hear my prayer for Jesus' sake. Amen.

(from *Little Visits: 365 Family Devotions.* Volume 2)

When I'm Angry

Holy Spirit, I am so quick to get angry and stay angry. Direct my eyes to Jesus' cross, that day by day I might know the high price He paid for my forgiveness. Amen.

(from *Little Visits: 365 Family Devotions.* Volume 2)

Dear God, I need Your help, God, because I have a very bad temper. ... I am really sorry for what I did. Teach me to remember that my family really does love me and forgives me, just as You do. Help me show others how much love I have. Amen.

(from *God, I Need to Talk to You about My Bad Temper*)

Dear Jesus, when I get angry, I forget about Your love. Help me remember that You died on the cross to forgive me and to give me Your love. When I want to hurt others, help me show Your love instead. Thank You, Jesus. Amen.

(from *God, I Need to Talk to You about Hurting Others*)

Jesus, who walked on the water,
Jesus, who calmed the tossing sea,
Come to the aid of Your frustrated child.
Won't You calm the anger in me?

For I feel sad, not glad.
I feel lonely and out of place.
I feel bitter, not better,
And I just want plenty of space!

I'm more upset with myself; you see,
For the fault is mostly mine;
It didn't have to be, you know
How could I be so unkind?

But words have a way of hurting,
And silence is even worse.
I pray help me say: "I'm sorry,"
For the sake of Your dying cross.

Peace is Your gift to us
And forgiveness Your command.
Now I lift this prayer of sorrow
For peace-sake, lend a hand!
Jesus, Holy One, Your will be done! Amen.
(by John Paquet)0

For Missions

Lord, bless the little children
In all the world, I pray;
Help everyone to love You
And do the things You say. Amen.
(from *Little Folded Hands*)

Jesus, thank You for the talents You have given me. I'm
glad You love me so much that You came to serve and save

me. Help me be great for You by serving others. Amen.

(from *Little Visits: 365 Family Devotions*. Volume 2)

Dear Lord, help me always to listen for Your voice. Give me the courage and the words to say as I witness for You. Thank You for being with me wherever I go. Amen.

(from *Little Visits: 365 Family Devotions*. Volume 2)

Dear Jesus, thank You for living and dying for me. Please live in me so I can love and help people just as You did. Help me tell others about You so they can live for You too. Amen.

(from *Little Visits: 365 Family Devotions*. Volume 2)

Dear Jesus, thank You for finding us and bringing us into Your kingdom. Help us bring home those sheep still missing from Your flock. Amen.

(from *Little Visits: 365 Family Devotions*. Volume 2)

Heavenly Father, thank You for sending Your Son to be the true example of a servant. Show us where and how You want us to serve You. Strengthen us to be Your faithful servants. Amen.

(from *Little Visits: 365 Family Devotions*. Volume 2)

Take my hands and let them do
Works that show my love for You;
Take my feet and lead their way,
Never let them go astray. Amen.

(from *Lutheran Worship*, 404:2)

When Traveling

Sometimes, Lord, the road seems long.
I'm not always very strong.
Anyplace that I might be,
Please, dear Lord, stay close to me.
In Your name I pray. Amen.

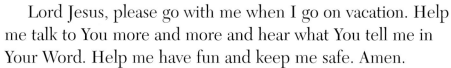

(from *My Christmas Prayer Book*)

Lord Jesus, please go with me when I go on vacation. Help me talk to You more and more and hear what You tell me in Your Word. Help me have fun and keep me safe. Amen.

(from *Little Visits: 365 Family Devotions.* Volume 2)

For my Country

God bless our native land;
Firm may it ever stand
Through storm and night.
When the wild tempests rave,
Ruler of wind and wave,
Do Thou our country save
By Thy great might.Amen.

(from *Lutheran Worship*, 497:1)

Father God, thank You for the country in which I live. Help me discover Your goodness even when people do sinful things. Send Your Spirit to create faith in Jesus Christ in the hearts of all people so we can share true peace. Amen.

(from *Little Visits: 365 Family Devotions.* Volume 2)

Lord of all creation, we thank and praise You for our wonderful country. In Jesus' name. Amen.

(from *Little Visits: 365 Family Devotions.* Volume 2)

Our God, our help in ages past,
Our hope for years to come,
Still be our guard while troubles last
And our eternal home! Amen.
(from *Lutheran Worship*, 180:6)

O God of love, O King of peace,
Make wars throughout the world to cease;
Our greed and sinful wrath restrain.
Give peace, O God, give peace again.

Whom shall we trust but You, O Lord?
Where rest but on Your faithful Word?
None ever called on You in vain.
Give peace, O God, give peace again. Amen.
(from *Lutheran Worship*, 498:1,3)

For Forgiveness

Father God, I'm sorry
For the bad things that I do.
Forgive my sins and bless me.
In Jesus, make me new. Amen.

Lord Jesus, sometimes we say things that hurt others. Please forgive us, and help us use our words in ways that please You. Amen.
(from *Little Visits: 365 Family Devotions.* Volume 1)

Loving Father, You are so good to us. Thanks for all the good things we enjoy in life. Thank You especially for the gifts of forgiveness and life with You. Help us live as Your children who belong to You. In Jesus' name we pray. Amen.
(from *Little Visits: 365 Family Devotions.* Volume 1)

We thank You, heavenly Father that Your love for us is always the same. You never grow tired of loving us, helping us, and forgiving us. We sin every day, and we need Your forgiveness daily. We are thankful that You are always willing to listen to our prayers. Make us truly sorry for all our sins. In Jesus' name we pray. Amen.

(from *Little Visits: 365 Family Devotions.* Volume 1)

Heavenly Father, forgive our sins for Jesus' sake. Help us stay away from those things that are not pleasing to You. For Jesus' sake. Amen.

(from *Little Visits: 365 Family Devotions.* Volume 1)

Dear Jesus, we know that our wrong behavior deserves Your anger. Thank You for loving us instead and forgiving our sins. Please take away all angry thoughts, words, and deeds, and help us treat others as You treat us. Amen.

(from *Little Visits: 365 Family Devotions.* Volume 1)

Dear Jesus, sometimes we hurt people because we are selfish and think only of our own fun. Forgive us, and empower us with Your Spirit to show kindness and forgiveness to others. Amen.

(from *Little Visits: 365 Family Devotions.* Volume 1)

"Have mercy on me, O God, according to Your unfailing love; according to Your great compassion blot out my transgressions. Wash away all my iniquity and cleanse me from my sin" (Psalm 51:1–2). Amen.

Lord Jesus, forgive us for the times we think too highly of ourselves. Forgive us for the times we try to make ourselves look the most important. Thank You, Jesus, for serving us and for helping us to serve others. Amen.

(from *Little Visits: 365 Family Devotions.* Volume 1)

When sins are forgiven, how glad are we!
Forgive me, dear Lord, for the sin in me.
I'm sorry for tearing my new blue coat.
I'm sorry for breaking my brother's boat.
I'm sorry for losing my dad's new tool.
I'm sorry for being so rude in school.
I'm sorry for not saying words like "please,"
For causing my sister to skin her knees.
I'm sorry for selfishly hogging toys
And keeping them only for my own joy.
Help me, dear God, be the best I can be.
Forgive me, dear Lord, for the sin in me.
When sins are forgiven, how glad are we! Amen.

(from *More Songs of Gladness*)

Please help my friend forgive my sin
And make us then what we have been—
Two friends who love like one. Amen.

(from *God, I've Gotta Talk to You!*)

I thank You, Jesus, You're my friend,
For You felt lonely, too.
Your friends ran off and left You and
Your heart was broken in two.
But You forgave them—every one—
And loved them even more.

Please, help me to forgive my friends,
For that's what friends are for. Amen.

(from *God, I've Gotta Talk to You ... Again!*)

O my Savior, help afford
By Your Spirit and Your Word!
When my wayward heart would stray,
Keep me in the narrow way;
Grace in time of need supply
While I live and when I die. Amen.

(from *Lutheran Worship*, 285:5)

Dear Jesus, sometimes I am afraid to tell the truth. Forgive me, Jesus, and help me be brave enough to always tell the truth. ... I am sorry. I love You, Jesus. Amen.

(from *God, I Need to Talk to You about Lying*)

Dear Jesus, You gave me so much love when You died for my sins. And I know You shared with me all the things that I have. I know it is wrong when I don't share. Forgive me. Help me share my things and especially share Your love. Amen.

(from *God, I Need to Talk to You about Sharing*)

Dear Jesus, help me use the ears You gave me. Forgive me when I think only about myself and do not care about others or pay attention to them. I am thankful that You pay attention to me and that You are not too busy to hear me. Thank You for loving me and for forgiving my sins. You really do care about me. And thank You for my ears. Amen.

(from *God, I Need to Talk to You about Paying Attention*)

Jesus, I know that cheating is a sin. Thank You for forgiving my sins. ... Thank You, Jesus, for helping me love others. Amen.

(from *God, I Need to Talk to You about Cheating*)

Jesus, forgive me for hurting [name]. I know damaging other people's things is always wrong. Thank You for loving me even when I am bad. Help me to love others, even when they mistreat me. Amen.

(from *God, I Need to Talk to You about Vandalism*)

Dear Jesus, I was wrong when I took something that was not mine; I know I hurt others when I steal. Please, forgive me. Thank You for dying for my sins. Help my life show that I love You. Amen.

(from *God, I Need to Talk to You about Stealing*)

Baptism

Thank You, God, for washing us clean in Baptism. Help us live to be more like Your saints, for Jesus' sake. Amen.

(from *Little Visits: 365 Family Devotions.* Volume 1)

We don't want to have sin in us, dear Lord. We want to be clean. But, Lord, we were born sinners, and we sin daily. Remind us of our Baptism and how You scrubbed us clean. Then give us peace in knowing we are forgiven. Amen.

(from *Little Visits: 365 Family Devotions.* Volume 1)

Dear Father, thank You for adopting each one of us in Baptism. Remind us often that You love us and care about us, even when we do wrong things. We know You forgive us because of Jesus. Amen.

(from *Little Visits: 365 Family Devotions.* Volume 1)

Lord and Teacher, thank You for washing away our sins. Thank You for the example You give us in Your Word. Help us by Your Spirit to live in humble service to others. Amen.

(from *Little Visits: 365 Family Devotions.* Volume 1)

Baptized into Your name most holy,
O Father, Son, and Holy Ghost,
I claim a place, though weak and lowly,
Among Your seed, Your chosen host.
Buried with Christ and dead to sin,
I have Your Spirit now within.

All that I am and love most dearly,
Receive it all, O Lord, from me.
Oh, let me make my vows sincerely,
And help me Your own child to be!
Let nothing that I am or own
Serve any will but Yours alone. Amen.

(from *Lutheran Worship,* 224:1,4)

Faith

Dear Father, we are sometimes distracted by the things of this world. Thank You that although we sometimes lose sight of You, You always keep us clearly in Your sight. In Jesus' name. Amen.

(from *Little Visits: 365 Family Devotions.* Volume 1)

Heavenly Father, give us a strong faith so we can stand firm against the temptations that surround us. Give us a faith that will be a shining light leading others to You. In the Savior's name we pray. Amen.

(from *Little Visits: 365 Family Devotions.* Volume 1)

Faithful Shepherd, feed me
In the pastures green.
Faithful Shepherd, lead me
Where Thy steps are seen.

Hold me fast, and guide me
In the narrow way
So, with Thee beside me,
I shall never stray.

Daily bring me nearer
To the heavenly shore;
May my faith grow clearer,
May I love Thee more. Amen.

(from *The Children's Hymnal*, 141:1–3)

My faith looks trustingly
To Christ of Calvary,
My Savior true!
Lord, hear me while I pray,
Take all my guilt away,
Strengthen in ev'ry way
My love for You! Amen.

(from *Lutheran Worship*, 378:1)

I am Jesus' little lamb,
Ever glad at heart I am;
For my Shepherd gently guides me,
Knows my need and well provides me,
Loves me ev'ry day the same,
Even calls me by my name. Amen.

(from *Lutheran Worship*, 517:1)

Trust

Almighty God, we thank You that Jesus Christ gave up His life and everything He had for us. Help us to trust and serve You with our whole heart. We pray in Jesus' name. Amen.

(from *Little Visits: 365 Family Devotions.* Volume 1)

I am trusting You, Lord Jesus,
Trusting only You;
Trusting You for full salvation,
Free and true.

I am trusting You, to guide me;
You alone shall lead,
Ev'ry day and hour supplying
All my need. Amen.

(from *Lutheran Worship,* 408)

Lord God, thank You that You do what You have promised at just the right time. Help us trust You and wait patiently for You to act. Amen.

(from *Little Visits: 365 Family Devotions.* Volume 1)

Thank You, Jesus, for promising to keep us close to You. Your love fills me with joy, knowing that You forgive me and have a place for me in heaven. Amen.

(from *Little Visits: 365 Family Devotions.* Volume 1)

Dear Jesus, thank You for coming into this dark world to bring us Your heavenly light. Help us to reflect Your light to others. For Your name's sake. Amen.

(from *Little Visits: 365 Family Devotions.* Volume 1)

Create in me a clean heart, O God, and renew a right spirit within me. Cast me not away from Your presence, and take not Your Holy Spirit from me. Restore to me the joy of Your salvation, and uphold me with Your free Spirit. Amen.

(from *Lutheran Worship*, p. 175)

Be our light in the darkness, O Lord, and in Your great mercy defend us from all perils and dangers of this night; for the love of Your only Son, our Savior Jesus Christ. Amen.

(from *Lutheran Worship*, p. 267)

There are lots of questions, God,
I don't have answers to;
So, help me always to believe
And put my trust in You.

I know You know the answers, Lord;
And, Lord, I know You care.
So, that is why I never doubt
You hear my every prayer. Amen.

(from *God, I've Gotta Talk to You...Again!*)

Praise

Beautiful Savior, King of creation,
Son of God and Son of Man!
Truly I'd love Thee,
Truly I'd serve Thee,
Light of my soul, my joy, my crown.

Beautiful Savior, Lord of the nations,
Son of God and Son of Man!
Glory and honor,
Praise, adoration
Now and forever more be Thine! Amen.

(from *Lutheran Worship*, 507)

Sweeter than the sweetest dream,
Warmer than the sun's gold beam,
Kinder than Mom's arms can be,
Wiser than from A to Z,
God, You're all in all to me.

Better than the talk of friends,
Gentler than my sister's hands,
Closer than the air I breathe,
Now and through eternity,
God, You're all in all to me. Amen.
(from *More Songs of Gladness*)

To God the Father, God the Son,
To God the Spirit, three in one,
Honor and praise forever be
Now and through all eternity! Amen.
(from *Lutheran Worship* 197:3)

Praise God, from whom all blessings flow;
Praise Him, all creatures here below;
Praise Him above, ye heavenly host:
Praise Father, Son, and Holy Ghost. Amen.